Contractions and Possessives

Kara Murray

PowerKiDS press.
New York

Published in 2014 by The Rosen Publishing Group, Inc.
29 East 21st Street, New York, NY 10010

First Edition

Editor: Amelie von Zumbusch
Book Design: Colleen Bialecki

Photo Credits: Cover Karen Roach/Shutterstock.com; p. 4 Sam Edwards/OJO Images/Getty Images; p. 5 Korpithas/Shutterstock.com; p. 6 KidStock/Blend Images/Getty Images; p. 7 Joe Stone/Shutterstock.com; p. 9 Maria Teijeiro/OJO Images/Getty Images; p. 11 Pressmaster/Shutterstock.com; p. 12 Darrin Klimek/Digital Vision/Thinkstock; p. 13 Creatas/Thinkstock; p. 15 Sonya Etchinson/Shutterstock.com; p. 17 Golden Pixels LLC/Shutterstock.com; p. 18 iStockphoto/Thinkstock; pp. 19, 21 Monkey Business Images/Shutterstock.com.

Library of Congress Cataloging-in-Publication Data

Murray, Kara.
 Contractions and possessives / By Kara Murray. — First Edition.
    pages cm. — (Core Language Skills)
 Includes index.
 ISBN 978-1-4777-0804-0 (library binding) — ISBN 978-1-4777-0982-5 (pbk.) —
ISBN 978-1-4777-0983-2 (6-pack)
 1. English language—Contraction—Juvenile literature. 2. Contraction—Juvenile literature. 3. Language arts (Primary) I. Title.
 PE1161.M844 2014
 428.2—dc23
                                          2012051005

Manufactured in the United States of America

CPSIA Compliance Information: Batch #S13PK5: For Further Information contact Rosen Publishing, New York, New York at 1-800-237-9932

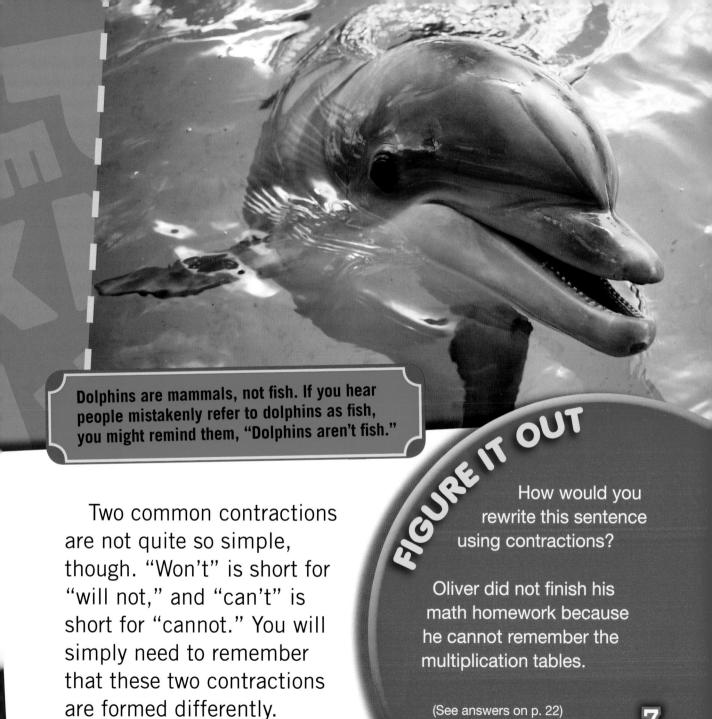

Dolphins are mammals, not fish. If you hear people mistakenly refer to dolphins as fish, you might remind them, "Dolphins aren't fish."

Two common contractions are not quite so simple, though. "Won't" is short for "will not," and "can't" is short for "cannot." You will simply need to remember that these two contractions are formed differently.

FIGURE IT OUT

How would you rewrite this sentence using contractions?

Oliver did not finish his math homework because he cannot remember the multiplication tables.

(See answers on p. 22)

7

"To Be" Contractions

"To be" is a special **verb**. It is central to our language, but its forms follow special rules. For example, we say "I am" and "he is" instead of "I be" and "he bes."

The contractions of **pronouns** and the forms of the verb "to be" are used often. They are "I'm" for "I am," "you're" for "you are," "he's" for "he is," "she's" for "she is," "it's" for "it is," "we're" for "we are," and "they're" for "they are." You can also use contractions if your sentence involves names. For example, you could write "Shannon's playing golf" rather than "Shannon is playing golf."

When someone thanks you, it is polite to say, "You're welcome." This is short for "You are welcome."

FIGURE IT OUT

How would you rewrite the following sentence using contractions?

I am happy to hear we are going to the movies tonight.

(See answers on p. 22)

9

Other Contractions

There are other verbs that commonly form contractions, including "will" and "have." To form contractions with "will," just add an apostrophe followed by "ll" to the pronoun. For example, "you will" becomes "you'll." You add an apostrophe and "ve" to form most contractions of nouns with the verb "have." However, add an apostrophe and an "s" with he, she, or it. After all, you say "he has," not "he have."

Chart of Contractions with "Will" and "Have"

Pronoun	With "Will"	With "Have"
I	I will → I'll	I have → I've
You	You will → You'll	You have → You've
He	He will → He'll	He has → He's
She	She will → She'll	She has → She's
It	It will → It'll	It has → It's
We	We will → We'll	We have → We've
They	They will → They'll	They have → They've

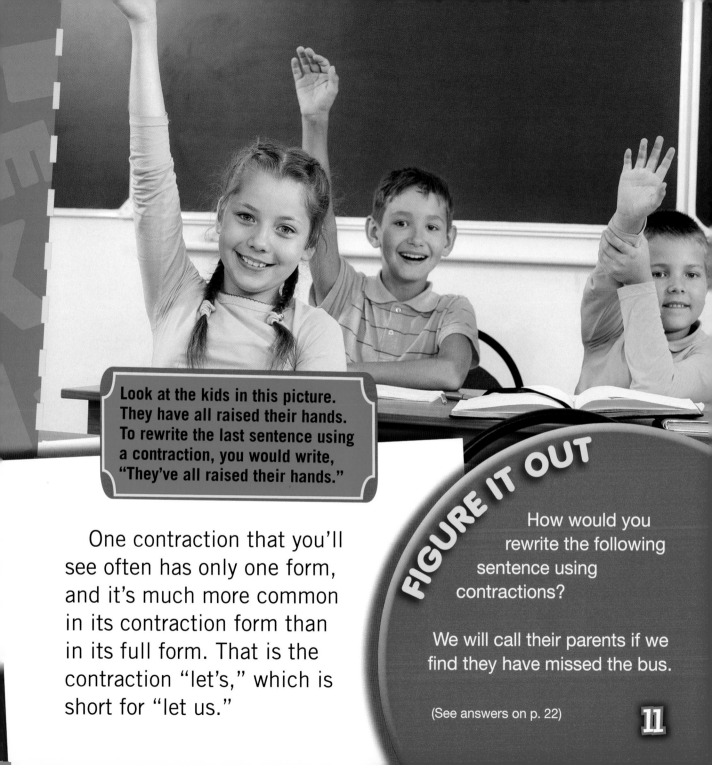

Look at the kids in this picture. They have all raised their hands. To rewrite the last sentence using a contraction, you would write, "They've all raised their hands."

One contraction that you'll see often has only one form, and it's much more common in its contraction form than in its full form. That is the contraction "let's," which is short for "let us."

FIGURE IT OUT

How would you rewrite the following sentence using contractions?

We will call their parents if we find they have missed the bus.

(See answers on p. 22)

Using Possessives

"To possess" means "to have." The possessive form of a **noun** or pronoun is a way of showing that something belongs to something else. To form the possessive of most **singular** nouns, you add an apostrophe and an "s." For example, the possessive form of the noun "eagle" is "eagle's."

Gabrielle's room is full of ribbons and trophies that she has won. "Gabrielle's" is possessive. In the first sentence, it shows that the room belongs to Gabrielle.

Some sentences have two possessives. "Liam's" and "Caleb's" are both possessive in the sentence, "Liam's tree house is Caleb's favorite place to hang out."

Another way to say that one person or thing possesses something is to use the word "of." For example, we could say, "Tammy's ball" or "the ball of Tammy." Which of these sounds more natural to you? The first is much more commonly heard and written.

FIGURE IT OUT

How would you rewrite the following sentence using the possessive?

Soup is the favorite lunch of my mother.

(See answers on p. 22)

Possessives with "S"

While possessives may seem easy, many people get confused about how to form the possessives of nouns that end in "s." Most **plural** nouns end in "s." A few singular ones do, too.

Most **grammar** experts say to just add an apostrophe and "s" to a singular noun that ends in "s," as you would for any singular noun. To talk about a cat that belongs to Charles, you would write, "Charles's cat." However, you may also sometimes see "Charles' cat."

To form the possessive with a plural noun, you add only the apostrophe. To describe a group for fathers, write "a fathers' group."

If you knew that this dog belonged to both of the boys in the picture, it would be correct to write, "The boys' dog is a golden retriever."

FIGURE IT OUT

How would you rewrite the following sentences using possessives?

This is the book that Mrs. Chambers says is her favorite. It has become the favorite of her students, too.

(See answers on p. 22)

Mine, My, and More

Did you know that there are possessive forms of all pronouns? For example, something that belongs to you is yours. Something that belongs to me is mine. "Mine" and "yours" are both possessive pronouns.

Possessive pronouns often take the place of other words. Let's look at the sentence "Those cookies are mine."

Chart of Subject Pronouns, Possessive Pronouns, and Possessive Determiners

Subject Pronoun	I	You	He	She	It	We	They
Possessive Pronoun	Mine	Yours	His	Hers	Its	Ours	Theirs
Possessive Determiner	My	Your	His	Her	Its	Our	Their

"Mine" takes the place of "my favorite spot" in the sentence, "The beach is my dad's favorite spot, and it is mine, too."

In it, the possessive pronoun "mine" stands in for the words "my cookies." "My" is a possessive **determiner**. Determiners are words that make the nouns that follow them more specific.

You may have noticed something different about the possessive pronouns and determiners. They don't have apostrophes! Never use an apostrophe with one.

FIGURE IT OUT

How would you rewrite the following sentence using possessive pronouns?

That wagon belongs to me and the other one belongs to you.

(See answers on p. 22)

17

Which Is It?

There are a few pairs of contractions and possessives that even adults tend to mix up. One is the possessive pronoun "its" and the contraction "it's." These two words are often confused because they sound exactly the same and are written almost the same. The only difference is the apostrophe.

This bird is flapping its wings. In the last sentence, "its" is possessive. Therefore it does not use an apostrophe.

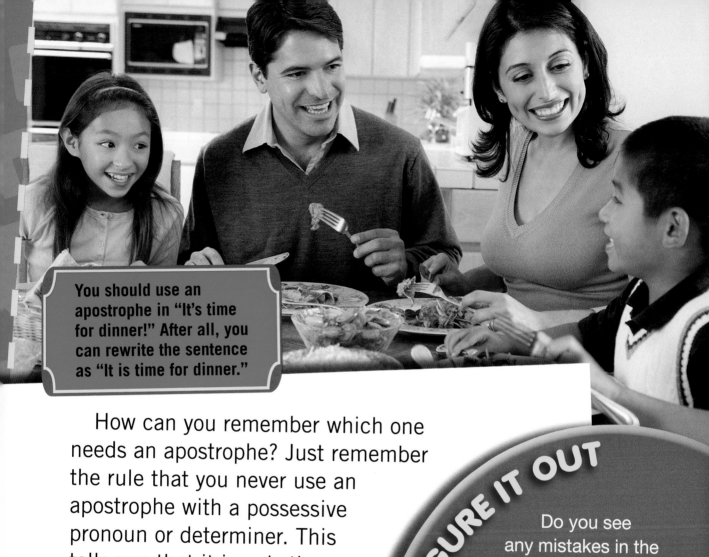

You should use an apostrophe in "It's time for dinner!" After all, you can rewrite the sentence as "It is time for dinner."

How can you remember which one needs an apostrophe? Just remember the rule that you never use an apostrophe with a possessive pronoun or determiner. This tells you that it is only the contraction "it's" that should ever have an apostrophe. If you can rewrite the sentence using "it is" instead, then "it's" is correct.

FIGURE IT OUT

Do you see any mistakes in the following sentences?

This is my mother's favorite TV show. Its on at 8:00 on Thursday evenings.

(See answers on p. 22)

Other Mixed-Up Pairs

There are other pairs of contractions and possessives that people often mix up, too. One is the possessive determiner "your" and the contraction "you're." Another is the possessive determiner "their" and the contraction "they're."

These pairs sound the same, so sometimes people forget which one to use when writing. You can remember the same rule that helped you decide whether "its" or "it's" is correct. Only contractions should have apostrophes.

Don't let apostrophes scare you! Now that you know when and how to use contractions and possessives, you can feel confident about using them in your writing.

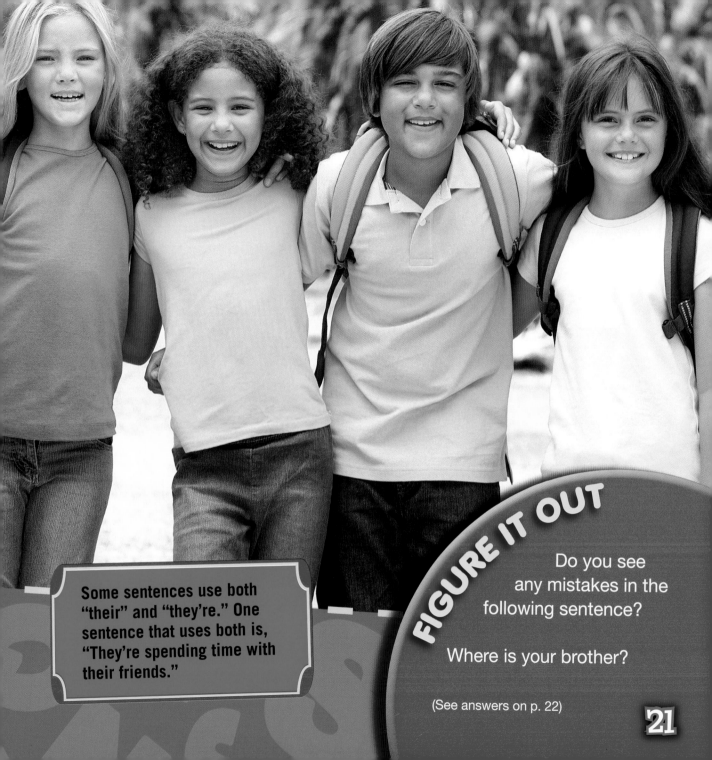

Some sentences use both "their" and "they're." One sentence that uses both is, "They're spending time with their friends."

FIGURE IT OUT

Do you see any mistakes in the following sentence?

Where is your brother?

(See answers on p. 22)

Figure It Out: The Answers

Page 5: "Couldn't" is a contraction and "teacher's" is a possessive.

Page 7: You would rewrite it as follows: Oliver didn't finish his math homework because he can't remember the multiplication tables.

Page 9: You would rewrite it as follows: I'm happy to hear we're going to the movies tonight.

Page 11: You would rewrite it as follows: We'll call their parents if we find they've missed the bus.

Page 13: You would rewrite it as follows: Soup is my mother's favorite lunch.

Page 15: Rewrite this one as follows: This is Mrs. Chambers's favorite book. It has become her students' favorite, too.

Page 17: You would rewrite it as follows: That wagon is mine and the other one is yours.

Page 19: "Its" should be "it's" in the second sentence because it is the contraction being used, not the possessive pronoun.

Page 21: That sentence is correct. The word you want is the possessive determiner "your," not the contraction "you're."

Glossary

apostrophe (uh-POS-truh-fee) A punctuation mark that looks like this: '.

contraction (kon-TRAK-shun) A shortened form of a word or words that uses an apostrophe in the place of missing letters.

determiner (dih-TER-min-er) A word or group of words that introduces a noun.

formal (FOR-mel) According to set rules.

grammar (GRA-mer) The rules of how words combine to form sentences.

informal (in-FOR-mul) Not following a special set of rules.

noun (NOWN) A person, place, idea, state, or thing.

plural (PLUR-el) Having to do with more than one.

possessive (puh-ZEH-siv) Showing or having ownership.

pronouns (PRO-nowns) Words that can take the place of nouns.

singular (SIN-gyuh-lur) Having to do with just one.

verb (VERB) A word that describes an action.

Index

Websites

Due to the changing nature of Internet links, PowerKids Press has developed an online list of websites related to the subject of this book. This site is updated regularly. Please use this link to access the list:

www.powerkidslinks.com/cls/cont/